THE ADVENTURES OF
THE JUNIOR DETECTIVES
BUTTERFLIES!

Written by Chantal Tomé
Illustrated by Anthony Santos

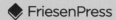

One Printers Way
Altona, MB ROG OBO
Canada

www.friesenpress.com

Illustrated by Anthony E. Santos
Copyedit/Proofread by Kelly W Hodgins

ISBN
978-1-03-831711-7 (Hardcover)
978-1-03-831710-0 (Paperback)
978-1-03-831712-4 (eBook)

*Juvenile Nonfiction, Animals, Butterflies,
Moths & Caterpillars*

Distributed to the trade by The Ingram Book Company

1

I dedicate this book to my amazing parents, who never let me give up on myself and always encouraged me in my dreams and goals. Thank you for always supporting me and showing me that I can make it in this thing we call life.

Hey there, Junior Detectives!

Welcome back for yet another new mission. Are you ready for our new adventure? Today we are going to investigate the life cycle of a butterfly and learn some fun interesting facts.

I am sure excited for our new adventure,
and I am sure you are too. So,

Let's Go!

Junior Detectives,

before we go on our adventure, what do we need? Yes, you are right! We need to put on our detective hat and detective jacket, and we need to take our magnifying glasses and our detective guide. Oh, wait! I seem to be forgetting something; do you know what that is? Yes, you are right! Our map! We wouldn't get far without our map, that's for sure.

Now where would we find butterflies,

Junior Detectives?

Let's take out our detective guide and see what it says. According to our detective guide, butterflies are mainly found in a tropical forest; they need warmth to survive. OK! Junior Detectives! How can we get to a tropical forest? Yes, you are right! We can take an airplane. Where would we find a plane? Let's look on our map and see what it says. According to our map, we can find the Junior Detectives plane at the airport!

OK! Junior Detectives, let's go!

OK! Junior Detectives,

we have made it safe and sound. Now are you ready to start our butterfly adventure? **Let's go!**

Hey, Junior Detectives, do you see what I see on the leaf? It is super-tiny. Let's take out our magnifying glasses to take a closer look. What do you think it could be? Let's take out our detective guide. Our detective guide says that this is an **egg** of a caterpillar. WOW! this is the first stage of a butterfly's life! It also says that most butterflies will lay their eggs on top of leaves. I wonder how the egg is staying still and not moving? Junior Detectives, do you know how? Yes! Let's look in our detective guide and see what it says. Our detective guide says that the female butterfly will make a sticky fluid that's like glue to help keep the egg in place. Here is something I didn't know: butterflies taste with their feet. So, they use feet to find food! When a butterfly is ready to lay eggs, she will use her feet to taste the leaf, and if that leaf would be good food for her eggs to eat once they hatch, she will lay her eggs there. **That is super-cool!**

Let's keep exploring, Junior Detectives. I wonder if we will come across a caterpillar!

11

Hey, Junior Detectives,

what is that on the leaf?

It's long, yellow, and fuzzy, and it looks like it's eating the leaf? You're right! It's a caterpillar. Did you know that a caterpillar is also called **larva**. What does **larva** mean? That is a great question, Junior Detectives; let's look in our detective guide! Our detective guide says **larva** is the stage after coming out of its egg before becoming an adult butterfly.

Here is something I didn't know; did you know that a caterpillar needs to eat 175 to 200 leaves before going into its next stage? I wonder if they only eat leaves? How can we find this out, Junior Detectives? Right! Our detective guide. Our detective guide says that caterpillars not only eat leaves, but they also eat flowers, grass, bark, twigs, and poop from animals. Well, that's quite the diet!

Junior Detectives: so far, we have seen eggs and caterpillars but no butterflies. I wonder why?

Do you know why, Junior Detectives? Those are all great guesses; let's look in our detective guide and see what it says. Our detective guide says that before a caterpillar becomes a butterfly it needs to form a **chrysalis.**

What is a **chrysalis**? That is a great question, Junior Detectives! A **chrysalis** is a temporary home that the caterpillar makes. The caterpillar will tuck itself in the **chrysalis** and then go through **metamorphosis** into a beautiful butterfly. What is **metamorphosis**? That is a great question, Junior Detectives! Let's take a look in our detective guide and see what it says. Our detective guide says that **metamorphosis** involves changes that some animals (like butterflies) go through to become an adult.

WOW! That is super-cool!

I hope we come across a **chrysalis**!

Look Junior Detectives:

do you see what is hanging upside down on the leaf? I wonder what could it be? Let's take out our magnifying glasses for a closer look! I think you are right, Junior Detectives. This must be a caterpillar, but why is it hanging upside down? Let's look in our detective guide. Our detective guide says that caterpillars will hang upside down on leaves or twigs and will make their silky, smooth chrysalis. Here is something I didn't know! It also says that it can take up to seven to ten days for the caterpillar to make its **chrysalis**. I wonder how long a caterpillar needs to stay in its chrysalis. What do you think, Junior Detectives? Great guesses, Junior Detectives! Let's look in our detective guide and see what it says. It says that most caterpillars will stay in their chrysalis for one whole week, and some will stay in their cozy chrysalis for three whole weeks!

WOW! That sure is a long time!

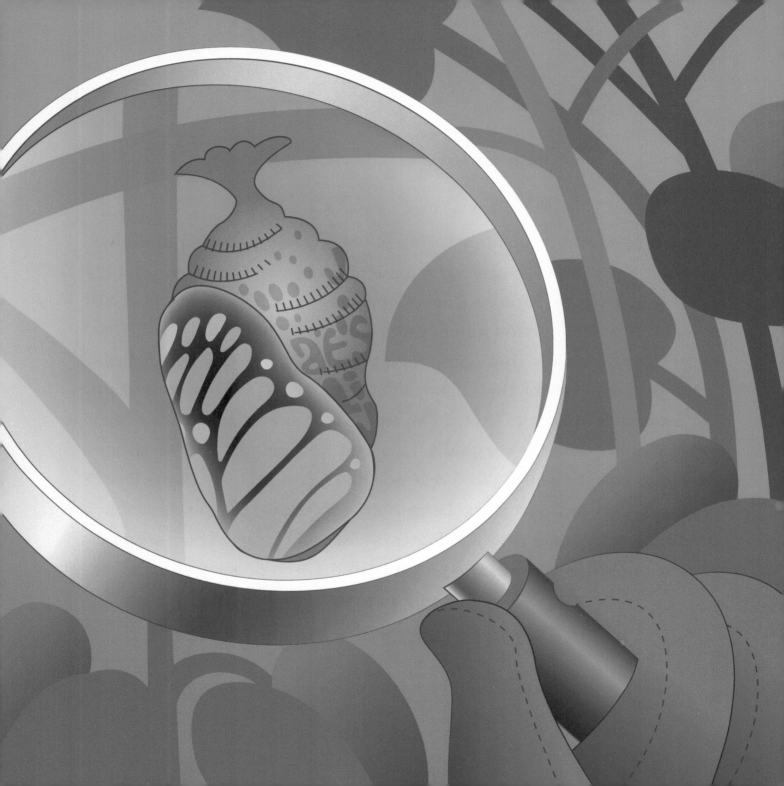

Hey, Junior Detectives,

I wonder what we will come across next! Look, do you see what I see? Can you see the butterfly through the chrysalis Let's take our magnifying glasses for a closer look. What do you see, Junior Detectives? Let's see what our detective guide says. Our detective guide says that once the chrysalis becomes soft and **transparent** (that's another word for see-through) the butterfly will use its legs to push a hole in its chrysalis. Once there is an opening the butterfly will crawl out of its chrysalis. That is super-cool!

I am sure we will come across some butterflies. I wonder which ones we will spot and what beautiful colours we will see!

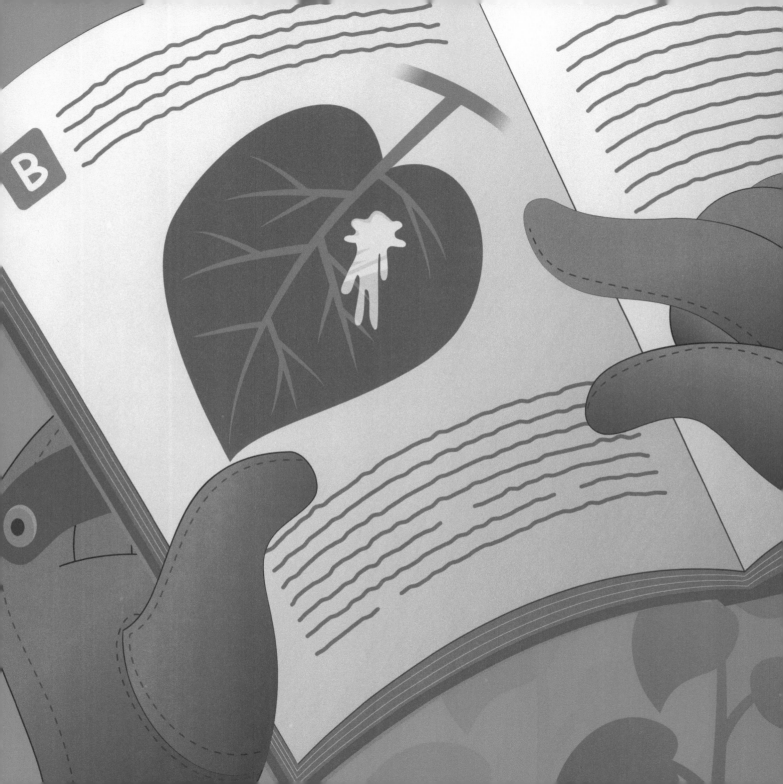

Hey, Junior Detectives,

I wonder how the butterfly got its name?

What do you think, Junior Detectives? Those are all great guesses. Let's see what our detective guide says. Oh! it says that butterflies got their name from how their poop looks. Dutch scientists noticed that their poop droppings looked like silky butter, so they started to call them **Butter-fly**.

That sure is a funny, silly fact, Junior Detectives!

Hey there, Junior Detectives,

do you see what is dancing up in the sky?

What colours do you see? You're right: bright orange and black. I wonder what we are looking at? Let's look in our detective guide to see what we may be looking at. Our detective guide says that this is a **Monarch** butterfly- it also says that monarch butterflies have white markings on their wings. Can you see them, Junior Detectives? How many markings do you see? Let's count together!

Junior Detectives, did you know that a **Monarch** butterfly is also called a **Danaus plexippus**? What does this mean? That is a great question! Let's look in our detective guide. Our detective guide says that **Danaus plexippus** is Greek for "sleepy Transformation" and that means that a monarch butterfly can hibernate and **metamorphize**.

WOW! I never knew that Junior Detectives. Did you?

Hey, Junior Detectives,

look over there at the trees by the river; it looks like this flutter (a group) of butterflies are looking our way. Do you see it, Junior Detectives? I wonder what butterfly this could be, what do you think, Junior Detectives? Those are all great guesses, so let's look in our detective guide. Our detective guide says that we have come across the **Morpho** butterfly. Oh, here is something interesting; did you know that their name **morpho** means changed?

Well, this is super-cool Junior Detectives! Our detective guide also says that the spots that we are seeing on the outside of the wing are called eyespots. This is to protect them from other insects or dangerous animals that may want to eat them.

Look, Junior Detectives! One is opening its wings; WOW, look at

the bright blue colour. Have you ever seen anything like this before? I wonder how the **morpho** butterfly gets wings this blue? Let's look in our detective guide and see what it says. Our detective guide says that their wings are not in fact blue. They have scales on the wings that create the colour blue by reflecting on other **structures** (like buildings or a bridge) of nature. That is so interesting! I never knew that.

Hey, Junior Detectives,

look at this beautiful butterfly that has landed on my glove.

WOW, this is super-cool!

Look at the beautiful dark purple and white pattern on its wings looks like a painting. Have you ever seen anything like this, Junior Detectives?

Did you know that butterfly wings are very **delicate**? What does **delicate** mean? That is a great question, Junior Detectives. Let's look in our detective guide and see what it says. Our detective guide says that **delicate** means it can break very easily. It says that a butterfly wing is very strong to be able to help butterflies fly, but if they are touched by us, we can hurt its wings and then it won't be able to fly. It also says that if you touch their wings their colours will fade away and their colours are used to protect them from predators. Here is fun fact: did you know that butterflies don't sleep? The way they rest is by closing their wings. I never knew that, did you, Junior Detectives? Let's place it on this flower and continue our adventure.

27

Look over there, Junior Detectives,

on the pink flower. Do you see what I see?

Do you see the butterfly, Junior Detectives? Look at the wings of this butterfly; you can see right through its wings. It looks like it's part of the flower; I wonder what kind of butterfly we are looking at? What do you think, Junior Detectives? Those are all great guesses. Let's look in our detective guide and see what it says; our detective guide says this is a **Greta oto** butterfly, also known as a **Glasswing** butterfly.

How do they make their wings see-through? Let's look in our detective guide and see what it says. It says that their wings look like glass because the tissue between their veins doesn't have colour like the other butterflies we see. That's so cool, Junior Detectives! Did you know that this helps the **Glasswing** butterfly camouflage (that's another word for hide) from other bugs or animals that may want to eat them.

That is super-cool! It's like they are doing magic!

Hey, Junior Detectives,

I wonder how butterflies drink nectar from the flowers?

What do you think, Junior Detectives? These are all great guesses! Our detective guide says that butterflies use their **proboscis**. That is their tongue. When they go to a flower, they will uncurl their **proboscis** and will drink the nectar. Here is something I didn't know, Junior Detectives; nectar can be hard to reach, so their tongues can be as long as a straw to allow them to reach the nectar.

That is cool, Junior Detectives!

Hey, Junior Detectives,
look over there by the trees!

Do you see those big wings? They look like bird wings. Could this be a butterfly? What you think, Junior Detectives? These are all great guesses. Let's look in our detective guide and see what it says. Our detective guide says that we are in fact looking at a butterfly, called the **Queen Alexandra's Birdwing** butterfly and it's the largest butterfly in the world. Junior Detectives, one has beautiful bright colours, and the other one has brown wings with patterns. I wonder why? What do you think, Junior Detectives? These are all great guesses. Let's look in our detective guide and see what it says. It says that we are looking at the female and male of the **Queen Alexandra's Birdwing** butterfly. Can you guess which one is the male butterfly? You are right, Junior Detectives! The bright colourful one is the male. Junior Detectives, did you see another difference between the male and the female? You're, right: the female is a little bit bigger than the male. Junior Detectives, our guide also says that they are **endangered**. What does **endangered** mean? That is a great question. **Endangered** means that one day there maybe no more **Queen Alexandra's Birdwing** butterflies. That is sad, Junior Detectives. I hope that never happens.

Hey, Junior Detectives,

did you see how fast that butterfly just flew by?

It looks like it's skipping and bouncing. I wonder if it is in fact a butterfly. What do you think, Junior Detectives? Let's try and catch up to it to have a closer look. Junior Detectives, here is one that has made its landing on a long piece of grass. Let's take out our magnifying glass for a closer look.

Junior Detectives, are you seeing what I am seeing? Its body is fatter than a butterfly and very fuzzy. I don't think this is a butterfly. What do you think, Junior Detectives? Yes, let's look in our detective guide. It says that we have come across the **Skipper Butterfly**. Here is something I didn't know, Junior Detectives; did you know that the **Skipper Butterfly** is the fastest butterfly, and it can fly faster than a horse can run.

WOW! That is super cool!

Hey there, Junior Detectives,
wonder what butterflies do for the Earth?

What do you think, Junior Detectives? Those are all great guesses, so let's look in our detective guide and see what it says. Our detective guide says plants in our garden need butterflies to help them produce more seeds and help them grow! How do they do this? What do you think, Junior Detectives? Yes, you are right: butterflies go from one flower to the next. While they are drinking nectar from the flower, **pollen** goes on their bodies. What is **pollen**? That is a great question. Let's look in our detective guide, Oh! It says pollen is a powder that plants make when they bloom. When butterflies flutter to another flower, **pollen** falls from their bodies and will pollinate other plants in our gardens. Here is something I didn't know! Did you know that **pollinate** means that the plants can now make seeds and reproduce.

That is super-helpful, Junior Detectives
and another reason why butterflies make us smile.

Junior Detectives-it's getting late.
We should head back to the Junior Detectives plane.
We sure have a long trip home. We had a great adventure discovering
fun facts about butterflies and learning about their life cycle.

I am glad to be home. We sure had fun on our butterfly adventure! We all learned some cool facts.

Until next time,

Junior Detectives!

Printed in the USA
CPSIA information can be obtained
at www.ICGtesting.com
LVHW061023041124
795331LV00023B/24